LEONARDO DA VINCI

MASTERMINDS

STEPHEN WHITE-THOMSON

B.E.S.

All inquiries should be addressed to:
Peterson's Publishing, LLC
4380 S. Syracuse Street, Suite 200
Denver, CO 80237-2624
www.petersonsbooks.com

ISBN: 978-1-4380-8934-8

All words in **bold** appear in the glossary on page 30.

Printed in China

MIX
Paper from responsible sources
FSC® C104740

Picture acknowledgements:
Alamy: The Picture Art Collection 7, Pictures Now 8, Dennis Hallinan 10, Digital Image Library 11, incamerastock 14, Classic image 16, Art Heritage 18, Picture Art Collection 24, Dennis Hallinan 29; Getty: Science and Society Picture Library 5 and 22t, Hulton Archive 9, ibusca 15, 19 (x3), Bettmann 20, Dorling Kindersley 22b, Fratelli Alinari IDEA s.p.A/Corbis Historical 25t, Print Collector 25b, DEA/A.DAGLI ORTI 27, Bettmann 28; Shutterstock Georgios Kollidas cover, HildaWeges Photography 4, Shutterschock 6, Janaka Dharmasena 12r, 21 (both), lolloj 12l, 13t, Anton Krestyaninov 13b, Japon Pinta 17, Jakub Krechowicz 26, 30, Resul Muslu / Shutterstock.com
All design elements from Shutterstock.

Every effort has been made to clear copyright. Should there be any inadvertent omission, please apply to the publisher for rectification.

The website addresses (URLs) included in this book were valid at the time of going to press. However, it is possible that contents or addresses may have changed since the publication of this book. No responsibility for any such changes can be accepted by either the author or the publisher.

All facts and statistics were correct at the time of press.

CONTENTS

Leonardo da Vinci was a brilliant artist, as well as an **engineer**, **architect**, and **sculptor**. He was a leading figure of the Renaissance, which was a period between the 1300s and 1500s when many scientific discoveries and great pieces of art were made. He was fascinated by how things worked, and observed them closely so he could understand them better.

This statue of Leonardo is in Milan, a city in the north of Italy. Leonardo spent some of his life working there.

During his lifetime, Leonardo filled thousands of pages of notebooks with writings and **sketches**. Some of these sketches show ideas for inventions that were not tested until hundreds of years later. It was almost as if he could see into the future!

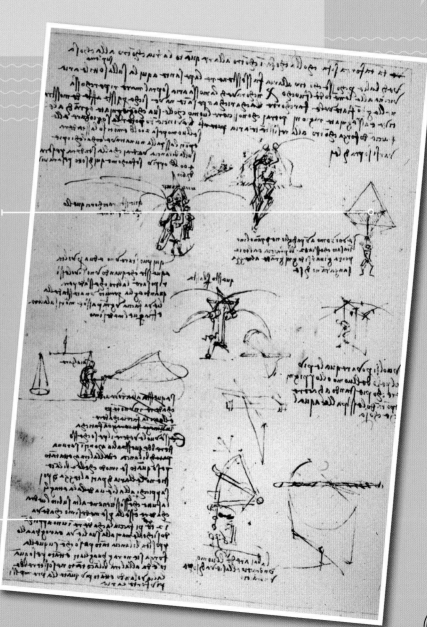

On this page from one of his notebooks, Leonardo investigated the idea for a parachute and how it might work.

Leonardo wrote the notes in his notebooks backward so you can only read them in a mirror. No one is sure why he did this.

Leonardo was born on April 15, 1452 near Vinci, in what is now Italy. His father, Ser Piero, was a lawyer. His mother, Caterina, was from a poor family. His parents were not married and did not live together. Leonardo spent most of his childhood living on the farm belonging to his father's family.

Milan

ITALY

Vinci

Florence

Rome

Leonardo's birthplace, Vinci, as it looks today. Leonardo "da" Vinci means Leonardo "of" Vinci in Italian.

When Leonardo was 14 or 15 years old, he became an **apprentice** to Andrea del Verrocchio. Andrea was a well-known sculptor and painter, based in Florence. He taught Leonardo the skills of sculpture, painting, and how to design machines. Leonardo soon became his best student.

Montelupo Castle

Valley of the Arno River

Leonardo used an ink pen to draw the countryside where he loved to walk as a child. He made this drawing in 1473, and it is the earliest surviving drawing that we know of that he did on his own.

In 1472, Leonardo became a member of the painters' **guild** in Florence. He stayed in Andrea's studio until 1477, when he set up his own studio in Florence. During this time, he created many sketches of machines. In 1481, he was asked by monks to paint *The Adoration of the Magi* (the Three Kings).

Leonardo never finished *The Adoration of the Magi* because he moved away from Florence.

Baby Jesus

Mary, mother of Jesus

One of the Three Kings who brought presents for Baby Jesus.

It is possible that this figure is a self-**portrait** of Leonardo.

In 1482, Leonardo moved from Florence to Milan, where he worked for the next 17 years. His **patron** was Ludovico Sforza, the Duke of Milan. Leonardo worked on many different projects as a painter, sculptor, and architect. He also spent many years working on a statue of Francesco Sforza, Ludovico's father.

These are some of Leonardo's sketches for the huge statue of Francesco on horseback. The statue was not finished because Ludovico was forced out of Milan by an invading French army.

Leonardo painted *The Last Supper* (c. 1495–8) while he was living in Milan. It is the only Leonardo wall painting that survives. Leonardo often tried new ways of working, and he used a type of paint that did not work well on walls. The painting has been **restored** many times.

The Last Supper is in the monastery of Santa Maria delle Grazie, Milan. It shows Jesus telling his **disciples** that one of them (Judas) will betray him.

Leonardo painted *Lady with an Ermine* (c. 1489–90). It is a portrait of Cecilia Gallerani, who was Ludovico's girlfriend. It is one of only four portraits that Leonardo painted of women.

Cecilia Gallerani

ermine

BODY SKETCHES

Leonardo is famous for his scientific studies of the human body. When he was an apprentice to Andrea, he studied **anatomy** with the help of the artist Antonio Pollaiuolo. Leonardo's detailed understanding of the body helped to make his paintings very lifelike.

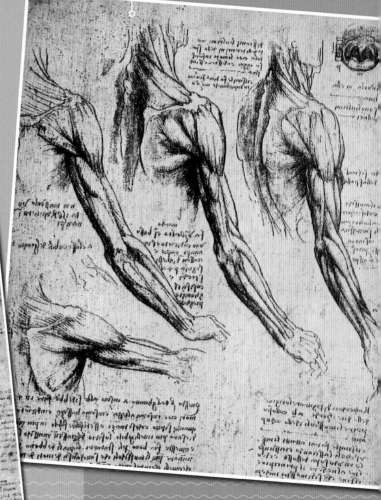

These sketches show the muscles in the neck, shoulder, and arm.

These sketches in Leonardo's notebook reveal the anatomy of the hand, with its bones and **ligaments**.

Leonardo used his excellent powers of observation to draw different parts of the human body: the skull and brain, the skeleton and the heart. He recorded these observations in his notebooks. He wanted to know, and show, how different parts of the body worked.

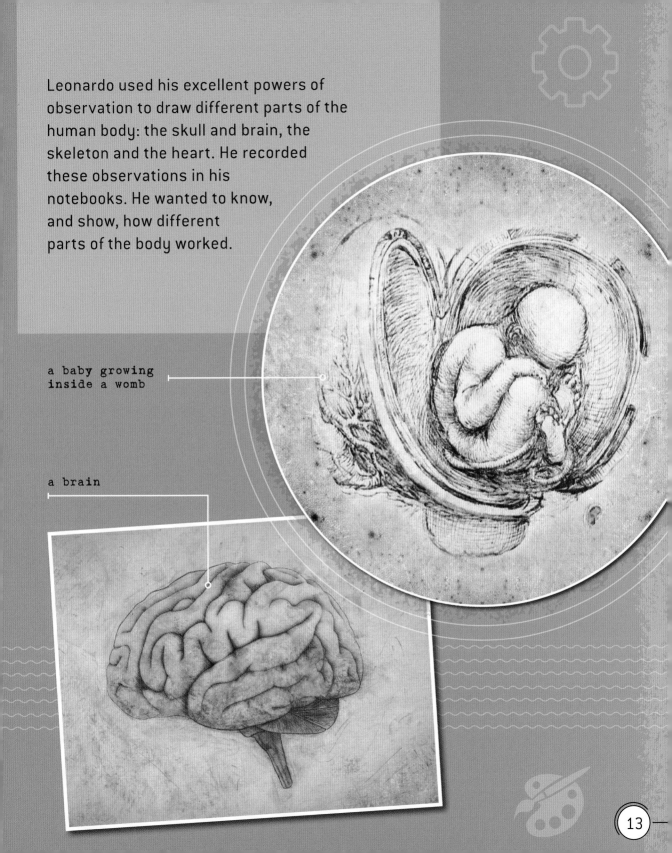

a baby growing inside a womb

a brain

When Leonardo returned to Florence in 1500, his range of skills was in demand. He was asked to work on lots of different projects that used his artistic and engineering talents. These included making a plan to build a canal to link Florence to the sea.

Leonardo drew *La Scapigliata* between 1500-5. "Scapigliata" means untidy in Italian, and refers to the woman's hair.

Leonardo worked for three years on a wall painting of *The Battle of Anghiari*. The battle was fought in 1440 between the armies of Florence and Milan. Florence won, so Leonardo was asked to create a painting to remember the victory, but he did not finish it. It has never been found, so it is known as "The Lost Leonardo."

This is Leonardo's sketch for part of his painting of *The Battle of Anghiari*.

THE *MONA LISA*

While he was in Florence, Leonardo started to paint the *Mona Lisa*, one of the world's best-known paintings. The woman in the portrait might have been Lisa Gherardini, the wife of a local businessman. Leonardo started the painting in 1503, but no one knows when he finished it.

Leonardo created the *Mona Lisa* using oil paint on a flat piece of wood. It is one of the first portraits to have a landscape as a background and to show the eyes looking straight at the viewer.

The *Mona Lisa* hangs in the Louvre Museum in Paris, France, in a room specially made for it. Because the painting is so precious, it is kept behind bulletproof glass to protect it.

Thousands of people visit the Louvre every year to see the *Mona Lisa.*

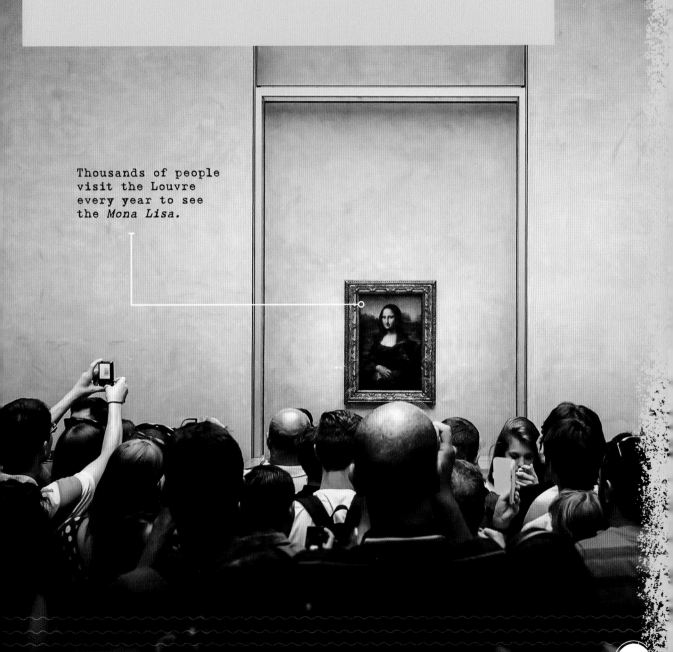

NATURE SKETCHES

Leonardo closely observed the natural world around him. He drew many sketches of animals, plants, and flowers. His drawings are very lifelike.

Leonardo's study of cats shows them playing, cleaning themselves, and resting. There is also a small dragon in the sketch: can you see it?

Leonardo sketched lots of horses. These were done as he got ready to paint *The Battle of Anghiari* (see page 15).

This sketch of a flowering plant shows Leonardo's eye for detail.

The trunk and branches of this tree look very lifelike in Leonardo's sketch.

Leonardo lived at a time when there were many wars. He was horrified by war, calling it a madness. But his patrons, including Ludovico Sforza, wanted to use his skills as a military engineer to help them win their battles. Since they were paying him, Leonardo had to do what they wanted.

This is Leonardo's illustration of a giant crossbow, which was designed to terrify the enemy.

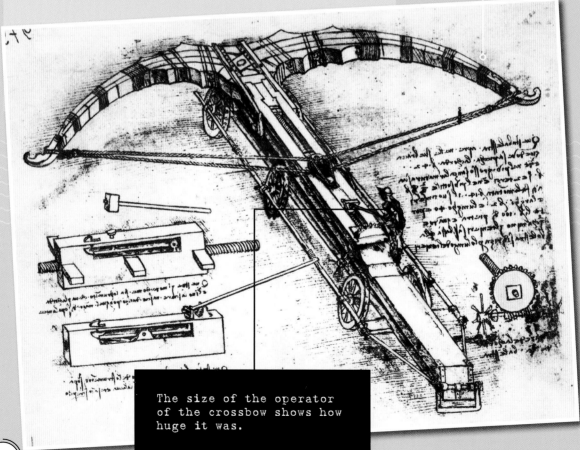

The size of the operator of the crossbow shows how huge it was.

Leonardo's sketches illustrate many different types of weapons: a sword-eating shield, fire throwers, and a multibarreled gun. Some of his sketches show the scientific workings of the weapons, such as how gears could help fire a giant catapult.

These sketches show a horse-drawn weapon with sharp knives, and an armored car with cannons that looks a bit like a modern tank.

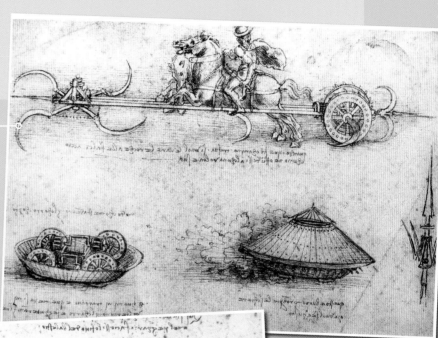

These sketches show an exploding bomb and how to protect yourself when fighting.

FLIGHT SKETCHES

Leonardo studied the flight of birds and observed how air flows over their wings to give lift and help them to fly. From this study, he believed that it was possible for humans to fly using flying machines.

Leonardo's sketch of a wing.

This modern illustration shows what one of Leonardo's flying machines might have looked like.

Leonardo investigated the idea that a machine with a large screw will lift off if it is turned with enough speed and force. His invention never got off the ground, but the basic science is similar to how a modern helicopter works.

Leonardo's sketch was done in 1493, about 450 years before a helicopter took to the air.

Leonardo's notebooks are full of drawings that show his talent for engineering. People then, like today, needed water to drink and to grow crops. He drew detailed machines to explore the best way to make water available for people to use. Leonardo believed that "water is to the world what blood is to our bodies."

Leonardo's drawings show his ideas for water-lifting machines.

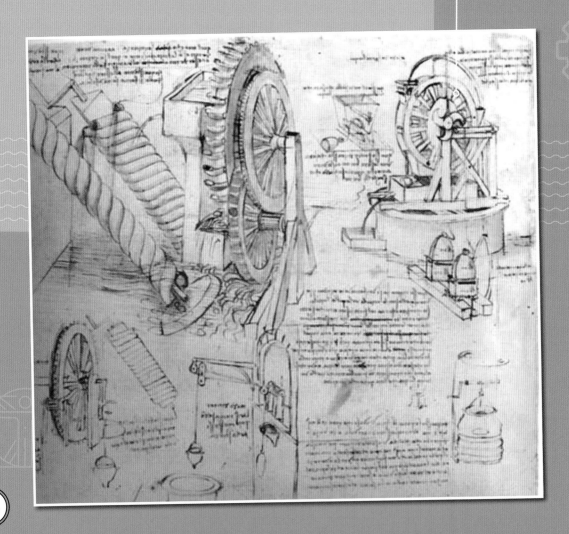

Leonardo designed bridges and sketched how they could be built to make them strong. He also worked as an architect, designing palaces and churches for his patrons.

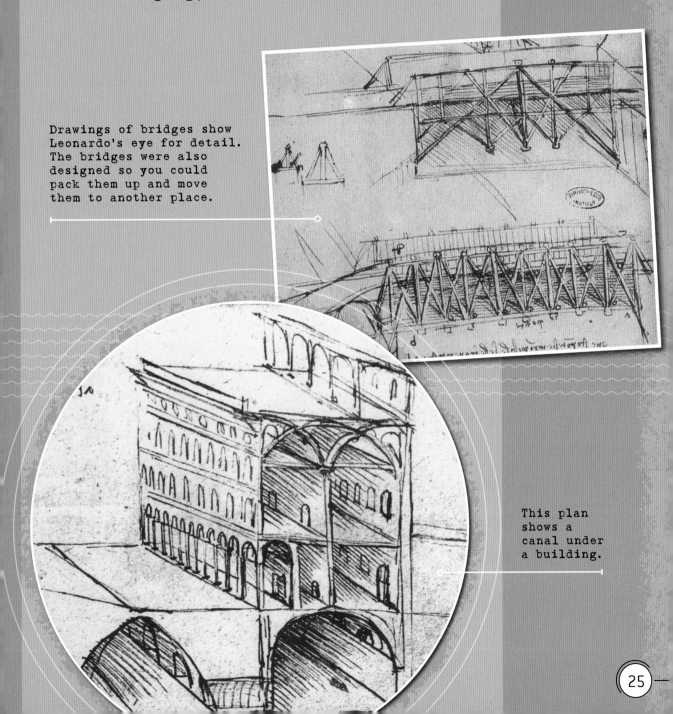

Drawings of bridges show Leonardo's eye for detail. The bridges were also designed so you could pack them up and move them to another place.

This plan shows a canal under a building.

In 1506, Leonardo moved back to Milan, where he lived for most of the next seven years. There are no finished paintings or sculptures from this time, but he filled his notebooks with drawings and notes on anatomy, machines, and studies of nature.

Leonardo drew this self-portrait in 1512 when he was 60 years old.

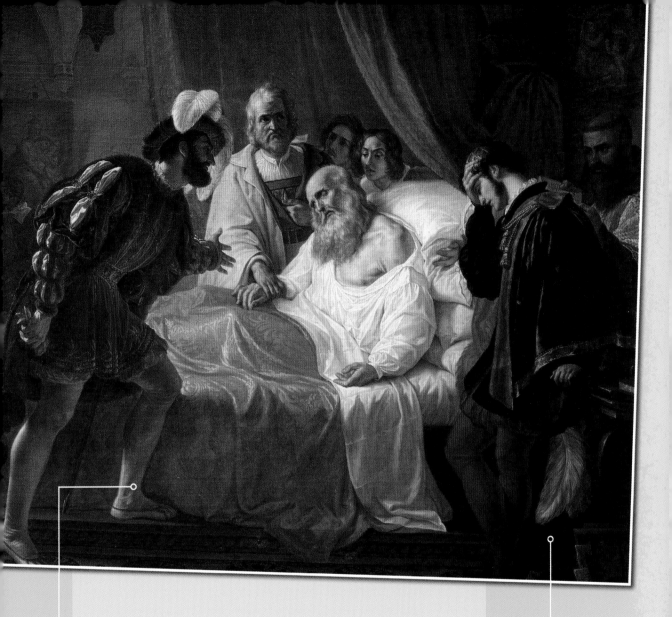

From 1513 to 1516, Leonardo lived in Rome. In 1516, he moved to France to work for the French king, Francis I, where he was called "First painter, architect, and engineer to the king." He died there on May 2, 1519 at the age of 67.

This imaginary scene of Francis I leaning toward a dying Leonardo was painted by Cesare Mussini in 1828.

REMEMBERING LEONARDO

Leonardo painted some of the most beautiful works of art in the world. But he was not just an artist. As his notebooks show, he was also a brilliant engineer and an architect. He was as comfortable creating the *Mona Lisa* as designing a flying machine.

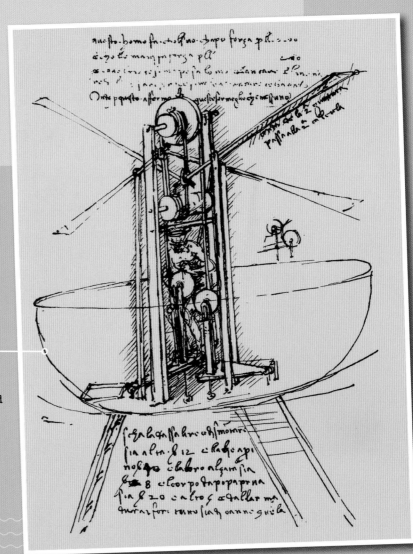

Leonardo imagined a flying machine driven by the strength of the pilot.

Leonardo lived at a time of extraordinary creativity. His curiosity and wide-ranging skills bridged art and science and were typical of the Renaissance. He once wrote in his notebook: "I never tire of being useful." Leonardo led a very busy life, working on lots of projects at once. He did not always finish them, but we have enough evidence of Leonardo's work to call him a mastermind—a genius whose legacy still inspires and influences us.

Mary, mother of Jesus

angel

Leonardo painted *The Virgin of the Rocks* around 1483–6. This painting is in The National Gallery, London, England.

John the Baptist

Jesus

GLOSSARY

anatomy: The study of the bodies of people and other animals

apprentice: Someone who is learning a trade or art from a skilled person

architect: A person who designs buildings and advises on how they should be built

disciple: A person who accepts and helps to spread the teaching of another

engineer: A person who designs and builds complex machines, structures, and systems

ermine: A weasel or stoat

guild: Like a club. Artists had to join an artists' guild if they wanted to open up their own workshop

ligaments: Tough bands of tissue that hold your bones together at your joints

patron: An employer

portrait: A painting, drawing, or sculpture of a person

restore: To return something to how it was to start with

sculptor: A person who carves hard materials into shapes, often of human figures

sketch: A rough drawing, sometimes done to prepare for a more finished piece of work

TIMELINE

1452
Leonardo da Vinci is born near Vinci, Italy.

1466 –77
Leonardo is apprenticed to Andrea del Verrocchio in Florence.

1472
Leonardo joins Florence's painters' guild.

1477
Leonardo sets up his own workshop in Florence.

1481
Leonardo starts to paint *The Adoration of the Magi*.

1482
Leonardo moves to Milan to work for Ludovico Sforza.

BOOKS

Who Was Leonardo da Vinci?
by Roberta Edwards
(Penguin Workshop, 2005)

**Magic Treehouse Fact Checker:
Leonardo da Vinci**
by Mary Pope Osborne and Natalie
Pope Boyce (Random House
Children's Books, 2009)

**Leonardo da Vinci: the Genius
who Defined the Renaissance**
by John Philip (National
Geographic Children's Books, 2008)

WEBSITES

**www.britannica.com/biography/
Leonardo-da-Vinci**
Read more about Leonardo's life

**www.theschoolrun.com/homework-
help/leonardo-da-vinci**
Top 10 facts/Timeline/Gallery

**www.kidskonnect.com/people/
leonardo-da-vinci**
Useful downloads and worksheets

1495 Leonardo starts painting *The Last Supper.*

1500 Leonardo returns to Florence.

1503 Leonardo starts painting the *Mona Lisa.*

1513–16 Leonardo lives in Rome.

1516 Leonardo moves to France where he lives the rest of his life.

1519 Leonardo dies at the age of 67.

INDEX

More titles in the **Masterminds** series

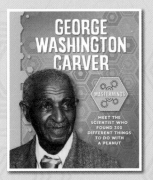

Who was George Washington Carver?
Childhood
Freedom
Getting an education
Farm studies
New crops
Peanut products
The sweet potato
Making a change
Colourful dyes
Honours
Later life
Remembering Carver

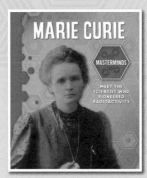

Who was Marie Curie?
Childhood
Studies in France
Meeting Pierre
Studying rays
New discoveries
Radioactive radium
Working hard
Family
Teaching and learning
The First World War
Later years
Remembering Marie Curie

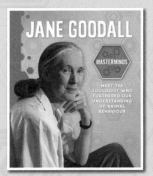

Who is Jane Goodall?
Childhood
Off to Africa
Ancestors and evolution
Living with chimpanzees
New discoveries
Back to school
Family
Inspiring others
Books
The Jane Goodall Institute
Activism
Celebrating Jane Goodall

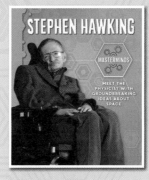

Who was Stephen Hawking?
Childhood
University days
Family
Space-time study
Black holes
A new voice
Sharing science
The future
Adventures
The Theory of Everything
Awards
Remembering Stephen Hawking

Who is Katherine Johnson?
Bright beginnings
Getting ahead
Teaching and family
A new job
Fighting prejudice
Into space
In orbit
To the Moon
Later life
Hidden Figures
Celebrating Katherine Johnson
A new generation

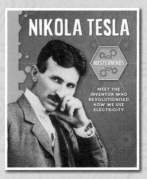

Who was Nikola Tesla?
Childhood
University studies
Bright ideas
Off to the USA
Tesla vs Edison
In the laboratory
Lighting the world
Free energy
Awards and honours
Later life
Remembering Tesla
Legacy

Also available: Rosalind Franklin, Leonardo da Vinci